SCHOLASTIC

W9-BEM-909

Vocabulary Packets
Greek & Latin Roots

by Liane B. Onish

NEW YORK • TORONTO • LONDON • AUCKLAND • SYDNEY
MEXICO CITY • NEW DELHI • HONG KONG • BUENOS AIRES

Teaching *Resources*

Hi, Mom!
Thanks, Judith!

Edited by Sarah Longhi
Content editing by Carol Ghiglieri
Cover design by Ka-Yeon Kim
Interior design and illustrations by Brian LaRossa

ISBN-13: 978-0-545-12412-6
ISBN-10: 0-545-12412-3

16   40   17

Contents

Introduction

The goal of *Vocabulary Packets: Greek & Latin Roots* is to introduce, reinforce, and provide practice in basic roots and *cognates* (i.e., words descended from the same roots). The activities are game-oriented to make learning roots fun. Students will have multiple encounters with each root and the related cognates to reinforce learning so they can "own" their new knowledge. Over five days, students will use clues to discover roots, find them in word searches, use them to complete crossword puzzles, uncover hidden bonus words and phrases in the puzzles, and use the words in sentences and review games. The rewards are the "a-ha" moments as students gain a deeper understanding of individual and related words and learn powerful tools to unlock the meanings of new words.

What the Research Says

Words are the name of the game. The more words you know, the more words you can speak, read, and write. The key to the game is learning as many new words as possible. Morphological awareness—the ability to identify meaningful parts of words (morphemes), including prefixes, suffixes and roots—can help.

▸ Morphological awareness improves decoding accuracy and fluency (Nagy, 2005). Decoding accuracy and speed improves when students can process larger chunks of text quickly. When students are able to recognize morphemes in increasingly complex words, reading speed increases, and students are better able to make sense of new and complex words in context.

▸ For every word known by students who can make use of morphology and context, an estimated additional one to three words should also be understandable (Nagy & Anderson, 1984). **Students who know roots can effectively double or triple their vocabularies!**

▸ Current research suggests that morphological awareness is the strongest consistent predictor of success for reading comprehension, reading vocabulary, and spelling.

▸ Morphological awareness impacts vocabulary growth (Nagy, 2005). Effective word-meaning instruction built on teaching key words, roots, and morphology results in stronger word attack and vocabulary skills.

▸ Research shows that morphological awareness contributes to vocabulary growth (Anglin, 1993) and that vocabulary knowledge contributes to reading comprehension (Stahl & Fairbanks, 1986).

When students encounter a new word, they may decode the word without understanding the meaning, or they may guess at the meaning using context clues. However, students with morphological awareness have a powerful tool for decoding and making sense of unfamiliar words. For example, if students know the prefix *mis-*, they will pronounce it automatically and they will understand how the prefix modifies the meaning of the base word. And if the base word includes a familiar root, such as *nom* (meaning *name*), the meaning of the unfamiliar word *misnomer* is more easily understood.

According to researchers, by the end of high school, the average student knows 80,000 vocabulary words. Clearly, not all of those words, not even a small percentage of them, were taught through explicit instruction. There are simply too many words and too little time. Giving students strategic tools to deepen their understanding of known words will help them unlock the meaning of new words. *Vocabulary Packets: Greek & Latin Roots* makes the learning fun and playful.

Words are power. Greek and Latin Roots are power tools!

How to Use the Book

Vocabulary Packets: Greek & Latin Roots covers 40+ roots, 150+ cognates, and 16 idioms, phrases, and maxims. Each of the eight units provides practice with five roots and cognates over five activity pages.

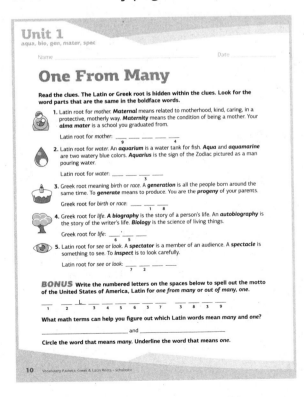

ACTIVITY 1

Unit introduction with cognate clues: Students use clues from three or more cognates to identify the target root. Includes a bonus Latin or Greek idiom, phrase, or maxim made up of letters from cognates containing the root.

ACTIVITY 2

Cloze sentences: Students supply the root that completes the cognate in a context sentence. Then they select a word and write and illustrate a sentence for it.

ACTIVITY 3

Word search: Students write the roots that match the definitions and then find them in a word search puzzle.

ACTIVITY 4

Crossword puzzle: Students complete the crossword puzzle with cognates of the target roots.

ACTIVITY 5

Student-made word cards: Students complete root definitions and list words that include the root. The word cards also include alternate root spellings. There is room on each card for four (or more) cognates. Units include at least three cognates for each root. Challenge students to find other words with the roots in the content-area and general reading (see the third Teaching Tip on the following page). On the back, students write a sentence and illustrate one word.

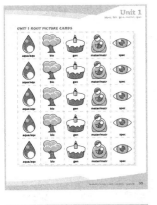

PICTURE CARDS

For each root, there is a postage stamp-size picture icon that students can tape to the fronts or backs of their word cards. Make one copy of this page for every five students. Give each student a strip of icons to cut apart and tape to their word cards.

REVIEW GAMES

After every two units, students can play a game to review and reinforce word learning. These games can be played with cognates from one or both units. For additional challenges, use words from more than two units, or add words from other subject areas.

Teaching Tips

▸ Duplicate Unit 1 and staple pages together for each student. Work through the lessons as a group. Encourage students to share their original sentences and drawings. Then have students work on subsequent units independently, spending five or ten minutes sharing their work in small groups.

▸ For page 1 of each unit, you might want to have students copy the cognates in a column to help them find the letters that spell the root in each word:

       maternal

       maternity

    alma **mater**

▸ Post the roots of the week on chart paper. Have students list cognates they find in their content-area and independent reading on the chart. Students can add these words to their word cards. Encourage students to use these words to make their own word searches and crossword puzzles for their classmates to solve.

Master List

UNIT	ROOT	MEANING	EXEMPLARS	PHRASES/IDIOMS
1 ▶	*aqua* (L) (also *aqu*)	water	aqua, aqualung, aquamarine aquarium, Aquarius	e pluribus unum (out of many, one)
	bio (G)	life	autobiography, biology, biography	
	gen (G)	birth	generate, generation, progeny	et cetera (and others)
	mater (L) (also *matr*)	mother	alma mater, maternal, maternity	
	spec (L)	see, look	inspect, spectacle, spectator	
2 ▶	*cogn* (L)	know	incognito, recognize, recognizable	cogito ergo sum (I think, therefore I am
	loc (L)	place	dislocated, local, location	
	nat (L)	born	innate, nation, national, native, naturally	ad lib (abbreviation o *ad libitum*, improvised literally, *according to pleasure*)
	ped (L)	foot	biped, pedal, pedestrian	
	sign (L)	mark	signal, signature, significant	
3 ▶	*aud* (L)	hear	audible, audience, audio, auditorium, inaudible	vice versa (conversely on the other hand)
	photo (G)	light	photocopy, photograph, photography, photographic, photosynthesis	ad nauseam (to an excessive degree; literally, *to nausea*)
	struct (L)	build	construct, construction, infrastructure, structure	
	therm (G)	heat	thermometer, thermos, thermostat	
	vis (L)	see	television, vision, invisible, visual	
4 ▶	*act* (L)	do	action, actor, activity, interaction, react	mea culpa (my fault)
	cycl (G)	circle	bicycle, cyclone recycle, recycling, unicycle	per diem (by the day)
	graph (G)	write	autograph, graphite, graphic, graphologist	
	mem (L)	recall	commemorates, memorial, memorize, memory, remember	
	tact (L)	touch	contact, intact, tactile	

NIT	ROOT	MEANING	EXEMPLARS	PHRASES/IDIOMS
5 ▶	*ast* (G) (also *astr*)	star	asterisk, astrolab, astronaut, astronomy,	tempus fugit (time flies)
	fac (L)	make	artifact, factory, manufactured	bona fide (in good faith, genuine)
	geo (G)	earth	geology, geography, geothermal	
	morph (G)	shape	amorphous, metamorphosis, morph	
	rupt (L)	break	bankrupt, erupt, interrupt	
6 ▶	*brev* (L)	short	abbreviate, breve, brevity	sub rosa (secretly, confidentially)
	cap (L)	head	capital, captain, capstone, decapitate	longa (long)
	ord (L)	row, rank	extraordinary, order, ordinal, ordinary	
	phil (G)	love	philanthropist, philosopher, philharmonic	Ars longa, vita brevis (Art is long, life is short; or, great outlives the artist)
	san (L)	health	insane, sane, sanitarium, sanitary, sanitation	
7 ▶	*log* (G)	word	apologize, dialogue, monologue, prologue	Scito te ipsum (Know yourself)
	max (L)	greatest	maxim, maximize, maximum	Caveat emptor (Let the buyer beware)
	nov (L)	new	nova, novel, novice, novelty	micro (very small)
	pel (L)	drive	compel, expel, propel, propeller, repel, repellent	
	strict (L)	draw tight	constrictor, strict, restrict, restricted	
8 ▶	*mand* (L)	order	commanding, command, demand, mandatory	Carpe diem (Seize the day)
	min (L)	small, less	mini, minor, minority, minimum, minus	Numero uno (number one)
	neg (L)	no	negative, renege, renegade	
	orig (L)	beginning	aboriginal, origin, original	term (end: exterminate)
	trib (L)	give	contribute, distribute, tributary	

Name _____ Date _____

One From Many

Read the clues. The Latin or Greek root is hidden within the clues. Look for the word parts that are the same in the boldface words.

1. Latin root for *mother*. **Maternal** means related to motherhood, kind, caring, in a protective, motherly way. **Maternity** means the condition of being a mother. Your **alma mater** is a school you graduated from.

   Latin root for *mother*: ____ ____ ____ ____ ____

                 9   4

2. Latin root for *water*. An **aquarium** is a water tank for fish. **Aqua** and **aquamarine** are two watery blue colors. **Aquarius** is the sign of the Zodiac pictured as a man pouring water.

   Latin root for *water*: ____ ____ ____ ____

             3

3. Greek root meaning *birth* or *race*. A **generation** is all the people born around the same time. To **generate** means to produce. You are the **progeny** of your parents.

   Greek root for *birth* or *race*: ____ ____ ____

           1   8

4. Greek root for *life*. **A biography** is the story of a person's life. An **autobiography** is the story of the writer's life. **Biology** is the science of living things.

   Greek root for *life*: ____ ____ ____

      6   5

5. Latin root for *see* or *look*. A **spectator** is a member of an audience. A **spectacle** is something to see. To **inspect** is to look carefully.

   Latin root for *see* or *look*: ____ ____ ____ ____

      7   2

BONUS **Write the numbered letters on the spaces below to spell out the motto of the United States of America, Latin for *one from many* or *out of many, one*.**

____ ____ L ____ ____ ____ ____ ____ ____ ____ ____ ____ ____
1   2   3   4   5   6   3   7   3   8   3   9

What math terms can help you figure out which Latin words mean *many* and *one*?

_____ and _____

Circle the word that means *many*. Underline the word that means *one*.

Name _____   Date _____

Cloze Call

Write the root that completes the unfinished word in each sentence.

1. In _____**logy** class we learned that if your parents have blue eyes, there is a good chance you will have blue eyes, too.

2. While on _____**nity** leave, Mrs. Zee visited our school with her new baby.

3. The _____**eration** that grew up during the Depression learned to do without many things.

4. Divers use _____**lungs** to breathe underwater.

5. The _____**tators** sitting in the upper decks are far from the action!

Use an answer from above in a sentence of your own.
Underline the word with the root in your sentence.

_____

_____

Draw a picture for your sentence to help remind you of the word's meaning.

Name _____ Date _____

Word Search: Mystery Root

Read the clues. Write the answers on the lines.

  1. This Latin root means *water*. ____ ____ ____ ____

  2. This Greek root means *life*. ____ ____ ____

  3. This Latin root means *mother*. ____ ____ ____ ____ ____

  4. This Latin root means *see* or *look*. ____ ____ ____ ____

  5. This Greek root means *birth* or *race*. ____ ____ ____

Circle your answers in the puzzle. Search down, across, and on the diagonal.

M	S	P	E	C
E	A	Q	U	A
T	C	T	E	T
E	R	G	E	N
B	I	O	A	R

BONUS On the lines below, write the letters you did not circle in order from left to right, top to bottom.

____ ____   ____ ____ ____ ____ ____ ____

This Latin phrase means *and so on*. It is usually abbreviated using the first three letters. Write the abbreviation on the line.

_____

Use the abbreviation in a sentence of your own.

_____

_____

Name _____   Date _____

Root Crossword Puzzle

Read the clues. Use the roots in the box below and what you know about them to complete the puzzle.

> **LATIN ROOTS** *mater, aqua, spec*   **GREEK ROOTS** *bio, gen*

CLUES

ACROSS

1. A sight to behold!

4. A tank fish live in

8. You and all the kids born around the same time

10. The state of being a mother

DOWN

2. A shade of blue

3. Having motherly feelings

5. To make or create something

6. A life science

7. One who investigates crimes

9. Children or offspring

On the back of this sheet, write a sentence that includes two or more words from the puzzle.

Name _____   Date _____

Word Cards

▸ **Complete the word cards.**

▸ **Cut them out and tape or staple them to index cards.**

▸ **On the back, illustrate one word for each root.**

▸ **Add the Root Picture Card (page 55) from your teacher to the front or back of the card.**

LATIN ROOT *aqua (also aqu)*

Means _____

Words I know with *aqua:*

1. *Aquamarine* means _____

2. *Aquarium* means _____

3. *Aqualung* means _____

4. Other words I know with *aqua:*

_____

GREEK ROOT *bio*

Means _____

Words I know with *bio:*

1. *Biology* means _____

2. *Biography* means _____

3. *Autobiography* means _____

4. Other words I know with *bio:*

_____

LATIN ROOT *mater (also matr)*

Means _____

Words I know with *mater:*

1. *Alma mater* means _____

2. *Maternity* means _____

3. *Maternal* means _____

4. Other words I know with *mater:*

_____

GREEK ROOT *gen*

Means _____

Words I know with *gen:*

1. *Generate* means _____

2. *Generation* means _____

3. *Progeny* means _____

4. Other words I know with *gen:*

_____

LATIN ROOT *spec*

Means _____

Words I know with *spec:*

1. *Inspect* means _____

2. *Spectacle* means _____

3. *Spectator* means _____

4. Other words I know with *spec:*

_____

Name _____ Date _____

I Think, Therefore I Am

Read the clues. The Latin or Greek root is hidden within the clues. Look for the word parts that are the same in the boldface words.

1. Latin root for *place*. An address is a **location**. A **dislocated** shoulder is one that is not in the shoulder socket. Things that are **local** are in the area.

Latin root for *place* is: ____ ____ ____
 2 1

2. Latin root for *mark*. Your **signature** is your name, your personal mark. A turn **signal** on a car marks or shows that the car will turn. Something that is **significant** is important or remarkable.

Latin root for *mark* is: ____ ____ ____ ____
 7 4 3

3. Latin root for *born*. **Natives** are those who were born in a certain place. A **nation** is made up of people who were born in that country. Talents and skills you were born with are **innate**.

Latin root for *born* is: ____ ____ ____
 5

4. Latin root for *know*. To **recognize** is to identify something you know. To go **incognito** is to hide so that you are not known or **recognizable**.

Latin root for *know* is: ____ ____ ____ ____

5. Latin root for *foot*. A **pedestrian** is one who walks. A **biped** animal is one that walks on two feet. You push the **pedals** of a bicycle with your feet.

Latin root for *foot* is: ____ ____ ____
 6

BONUS Write the numbered letters in the spaces below to spell out the Latin phrase that means *I think, therefore I am.*

____ ____ ____ ____ ____ ____ ____ R ____ ____ ____ U M
 1 2 3 4 5 2 6 3 2 7

BONUS BONUS What prefix means *two?* _____

Write the two words in the clues that have the prefix that means *two*:

_____ and _____

Name _____   Date _____

Cloze Call

Write the root that completes the unfinished word in each sentence.

1. A bicycle built for two has two sets of _____**als**.

2. The screaming fans never knew that the person wearing a wig and big sunglasses was their favorite movie star traveling **in**_____**ito**.

3. John Hancock's _____**ature** on the Declaration of Independence is the largest name on the document.

4. The surgeons gave the patient a _____**al** anesthetic instead of a general one that would have knocked him out.

5. The things you do easily are things that come _____**urally**.

Use an answer from above in a sentence of your own.
Underline the word with the root in your sentence.

_____

_____

Draw a picture for your sentence to help remind you of the word's meaning.

Name _____   Date _____

Word Search: Mystery Root

Read the clues. Write the answers on the lines.

1. This Latin root means *know.* ____ ____ ____ ____

2. This Latin root means *mark.* ____ ____ ____ ____

3. This Latin root means *foot.* ____ ____ ____

4. This Latin root means *place.* ____ ____ ____

5. This Latin root means *born.* ____ ____ ____

Circle your answers in the puzzle. Search down, across, and on the diagonal.

S	A	D	N	L
L	I	G	A	P
O	O	G	T	E
C	I	B	N	D

BONUS On the lines below, write the letters you did not circle in order from left to right, top to bottom.

____ ____   ____ ____ ____

This abbreviated Latin phrase means *to make things up on the fly, off the cuff—to improvise.* In Latin, it literally means *according to pleasure.* To see the full Latin phrase, add the letters *i-t-u-m* to the end of the second word.

Use the abbreviation in a sentence of your own.

_____

_____

Name _____   Date _____

Root Crossword Puzzle

Read the clues. Use the roots in the box below and what you know about them to complete the puzzle.

> **LATIN ROOTS** *cogn, nat, sign*   **GREEK ROOTS** *loc, ped*

CLUES

ACROSS

4. To know something when you see it

6. A country

8. A talent or quality that you were born with is _____

9. Able to be identified

10. Moved or forced a bone out of the joint it fits in

DOWN

1. One that walks on two feet

2. Nearby

3. Important or noteworthy

5. A person walking along the street

7. A sign used to communicate

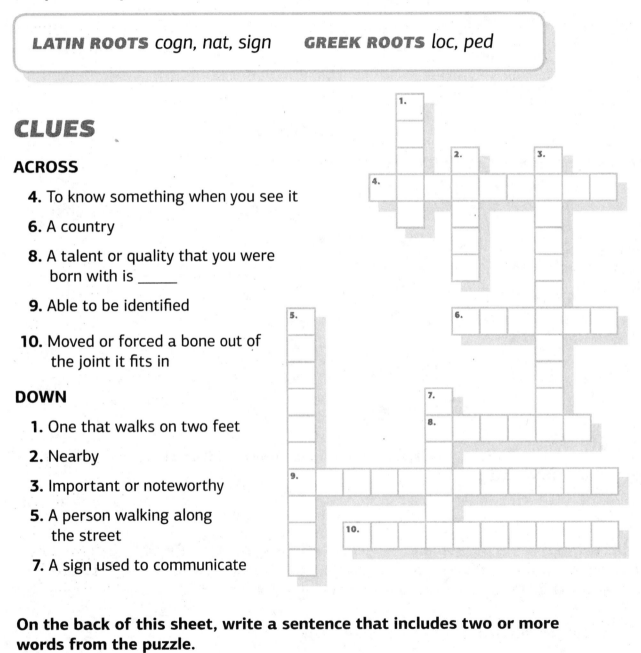

On the back of this sheet, write a sentence that includes two or more words from the puzzle.

Name _____ Date _____

Word Cards

▸ **Complete the word cards.**

▸ **Cut them out and tape or staple them to index cards.**

▸ **On the back, illustrate one word for each root.**

▸ **Add the Root Picture Card (page 56) from your teacher to the front or back of the card.**

LATIN ROOT *cogn*

Means _____

Words I know with *cogn*:

1. *Recognize* means _____

2. *Incognito* means _____

3. *Recognizable* means _____

4. Other words I know with cogn:

_____

GREEK ROOT *loc*

Means _____

Words I know with *loc*:

1. *Local* means _____

2. *Location* means _____

3. *Dislocate* means _____

4. Other words I know with *loc*:

_____

LATIN ROOT *nat*

Means _____

Words I know with *nat*:

1. *Nation* means _____

2. *Innate* means _____

3. *National* means _____

4. Other words I know with *nat*:

_____

GREEK ROOT *ped*

Means _____

Words I know with *ped*:

1. *Biped* means _____

2. *Pedestrian* means _____

3. *Pedal* means _____

4. Other words I know with *ped*:

_____

LATIN ROOT *sign*

Means _____

Words I know with *sign*:

1. *Signal* means _____

2. *Signature* means _____

3. *Significant* means _____

4. Other words I know with *sign*:

_____

Cloze Concentration

SKILL Identify cognates and roots
NUMBER OF PLAYERS Pairs
OBJECT OF THE GAME Match the cognate that completes a
cloze sentence and name the root

MAKE THE GAME CARDS

1. On card stock, make three copies of the blank game cards (page 54) for each pair of players. Have students cut the cards apart. (You can also hand out 30 index cards to each pair.)

2. Divvy up the cards so that each player has seven pairs. Players select seven cognates from their Unit Word Cards (pages 14 and 19) and write each one on a card. On the rest of the cards, they write cloze sentences to go with each of the cognates. Where the cognate would appear in the sentence, have students draw a box, as shown below.

MATERNITY	After the twins were born, Ms. Larsen took three months ☐ leave.

Write "Wild Card" at the top of the remaining two cards.

3. Students review each other's cloze sentences and cognates to be sure they are correct. Each pair of students should have made 30 game cards—14 sets of cognates and cloze sentences, and two Wild Cards.

PLAY THE GAME

1. Pairs of players mix up their game cards, place them in an envelope, and initial the envelope. Have pairs switch envelopes with another pair of players so that each game is played with cards other students have made. Players mix up the cards and place them facedown in a 5 x 6 array.

2. Play Concentration. The first player turns over two cards. If the cards show a cognate and a cloze sentence that the cognate completes, the player then identifies the root and its meaning. If correct, the player keeps the cards, and turns over two more cards. If the player turns over a Wild Card, he or she may write a cognate or a sentence to make a pair.

3. If the cards don't match, or the player incorrectly defines the root and its meaning, the cards are turned facedown for the second player's turn.

4. The player with the most cards wins.

Name _____   Date _____

On the Other Hand...

Read the clues. The Latin or Greek root is hidden within the clues. Look for the word parts that are the same in the boldface words.

1. Another Latin root for *see*. A **television** transports visual images into your home. **Vision** is your sense of sight. Something that cannot be seen is **invisible**.

Latin root for *see*: ____ ____ ____
                        1   2

2. Greek root for *heat*. An oral **thermometer** takes your internal temperature. A **thermos** keeps heat in. Raise or lower the **thermostat** to change the temperature indoors.

Greek root for *heat*: ____ ____ ____ ____ ____
                                    4

3. Latin root for *build*. A building is a **structure**. A place where a building is being built is a **construction** site. The **infrastructure** is the underlying inner framework of a building or system.

Latin root for *build*: ____ ____ ____ ____ ____ ____
                         6   5   3

4. Latin root for *hear*. The people who go a concert make up the **audience**. You listen to **audio** tracks through earphones. Something that is loud enough to hear is **audible**.

Latin root for *hear*: ____ ____ ____
                        7

5. Greek root for *light*. A **photograph** is a picture made with light-sensitive film. Green plants use **photosynthesis** to turn sunlight, water, and air into food to grow. A **photocopy** machine uses light to make copies.

Greek root for *light*: ____ ____ ____ ____ ____

BONUS Write the numbered letters in the spaces below to spell out the Latin phrase that means *conversely* or *on the other hand*.

____ ____ ____ ____   ____ ____ ____ ____ ____
 1   2   3   4   1   4   5   6   7

Use two roots to finish the sentence:

Movies are my favorite ____ ____ ____ _i_ _o_ ____ ____ _u_ _a_ _l_
form of entertainment.

Name _____ Date _____

Cloze Call

Write the root that completes the unfinished word in each sentence.

1. Those who look terrific in pictures are very _____**genic**.

2. If I had X-ray _____**ion**, I could see through walls.

3. The room was too cold so he turned up the _____**ostat**.

4. Little kids like to **con**_____ towers out of blocks.

5. The volume was so low it was **in**_____**ible**.

Use an answer from above in a sentence of your own.
Underline the word with the root in your sentence.

_____

_____

Draw a picture for your sentence to help remind you of the word's meaning.

Name _____   Date _____

Word Search: Mystery Idiom

Read the clues. Write the answers on the lines.

1. This Greek root means *heat*. ___ ___ ___ ___ ___

2. This Latin root means *build*. ___ ___ ___ ___ ___ ___

3. This Greek root means *light*. ___ ___ ___ ___ ___

4. This Latin root means *hear*. ___ ___ ___

5. This Latin root means *see*. ___ ___ ___

Circle your answers in the puzzle. Search down, across, and on the diagonal.

S	A	D	N	P
T	V	I	S	H
R	A	U	D	O
U	A	U	S	T
C	E	A	M	O
T	H	E	R	M

BONUS On the lines below, write the letters you did not circle in order from left to right, top to bottom.

___ ___   ___ ___ ___ ___ ___ ___ ___

This Latin idiom literally means "to the point of nausea," implying "to an excessive degree." Use the idiom in a sentence.

_____

_____

Name _____   Date _____

Root Crossword Puzzle

Read the clues. Use the roots in the box below and what you know about them to complete the puzzle.

LATIN ROOTS *aud, struct, vis*   **GREEK ROOTS** *photo, therm*

CLUES

ACROSS

1. This art form requires a camera.

3. I wear glasses to correct this.

4. This will keep soup hot on a cold day.

5. What you can't see is this.

8. A building

10. Cranes, diggers and other tools are used in this.

DOWN

2. The whole school met for an assembly here.

6. A duplicate

7. This will tell you if you have a fever.

9. Listen to this.

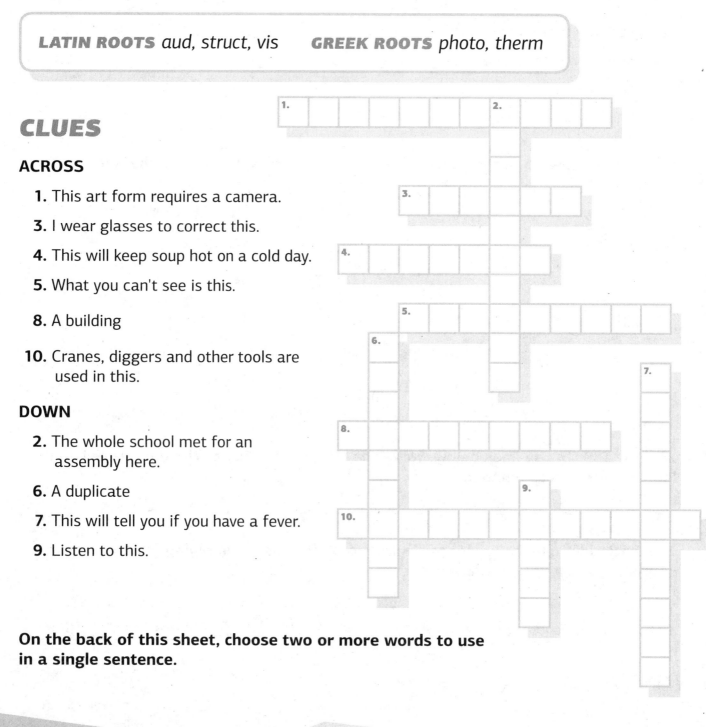

On the back of this sheet, choose two or more words to use in a single sentence.

Name _____   Date _____

Word Cards

> ▸ **Complete the word cards.**
>
> ▸ **Cut them out and tape or staple them to index cards.**
>
> ▸ **On the back, illustrate one word for each root.**
>
> ▸ **Add the Root Picture Card (page 57) from your teacher to the front or back of the card.**

LATIN ROOT aud

Means _____

Words I know with *aud:*

1. *Audience* means _____

2. *Audio* means _____

3. *Auditorium* means _____

4. Other words I know with *aud:*

_____

GREEK ROOT photo

Means _____

Words I know with *photo:*

1. *Photocopy* means _____

2. *Photography* means _____

3. *Photosynthesis* means _____

4. Other words I know with *photo:*

_____

GREEK ROOT therm

Means _____

Words I know with *therm:*

1. *Thermometer* means _____

2. *Thermos* means _____

3. *Thermostat* means _____

4. Other words I know with *therm:*

_____

LATIN ROOT struct

Means _____

Words I know with *struct:*

1. *Structure* means _____

2. *Construct* means _____

3. *Infrastructure* means _____

4. Other words I know with *struct:*

_____

LATIN ROOT vis

Means _____

Words I know with *vis:*

1. *Vision* means _____

2. *Invisible* means _____

3. *Visual* means _____

4. Other words I know with *vis:*

Name _____   Date _____

My Bad!

Read the clues. The Latin or Greek root is hidden within the clues. Look for the word parts that are the same in the boldface words.

1. Greek root for *circle*. A **unicycle** has one wheel. To use things again is to **recycle** them. A **cyclone** is a storm with circling winds.

Greek root for *circle*: ____ ____ ____ ____

　　　　　　　　　　　　　　　　　5

2. Latin root for *do*. An **activity** is something you do. **Interaction** is communication between two or more people or things. To **react** is to do something or respond to an **action** by someone or something else.

Latin root for *do*: ____ ____ ____

　　　　　　　　　　　3

3. Latin root for *recall*. To **remember** means to retain or recall knowledge. A **memorial** is a structure that honors the **memory** of a person or event.

Greek root for *recall*: ____ ____ ____

　　　　　　　　　　　　1　　2

4. Latin root for *touch*. Things in **contact** are things that touch. Your sense of touch is your **tactile** sense. Something that is **intact** is whole, with all the parts together.

Greek root for *touch*: ____ ____ ____ ____

　　　　　　　　　　　　　7　　4

5. Greek root for *write*. An **autograph** is your written name, your signature. The lead in a pencil is **graphite**. A chart or diagram in a book is a **graphic** element.

Latin root for *write*: ____ ____ ____ ____ ____

　　　　　　　　　　　　　　　　6

BONUS Write the numbered letters on the spaces below to spell out the Latin phrase that means *my fault*.

____ ____ ____ ____ U̲ ____ ____ ____

　1　　2　　3　　　4　　　5　　6　　7

BONUS BONUS What genre of books includes the Latin root for *life* plus one of the roots in this unit?

____ ____ ____ ____ ____ ____ ____ ____ ____

What does the word literally mean? _____

Name _____   Date _____

Cloze Call

Write the root that completes the unfinished word in each sentence.

1. That ringtone means my mom is trying to **con**_____ me.

2. Put the old newspapers in the **re**_____**ing** bin.

3. This statue **com**_____**orates** the end of a great war.

4. Nowadays, _____**ors** must also know how to sing and dance.

5. Can a _____**ologist** really tell all about you from your handwriting?

Use an answer from above in a sentence of your own.
Underline the word with the root in your sentence.

_____

_____

Draw a picture for your sentence to help remind you of the word's meaning.

Name _____   Date _____

Word Search: Mystery Root

Read the clues. Write the answers on the lines.

1. This Latin root means *do.* ____ ____ ___

2. This Greek root means *write.* ____ ____ ____ ____ ____

3. This Greek root means *circle.* ____ ____ ____ ____

4. This Latin root means *recall.* ____ ____ ___

5. This Latin root means *touch.* ____ ____ ____ ____

Circle your answers in the puzzle. Search down, across, and on the diagonal.

P	M	E	M	E	C
G	R	A	P	H	Y
T	A	C	T	R	C
D	I	T	E	M	L

BONUS On the lines below, write the letters you did not circle in order from left to right, top to bottom.

____ ____ ____   ____ ____ ____ ____

This Latin phrase means "by the day." What kinds of work might be paid one day at a time? _____

Use the idiom in a sentence.

_____

_____

Name _____   Date _____

Root Crossword Puzzle

Read the clues. Use the roots in the box below and what you know about them to complete the puzzle.

LATIN ROOTS *act, mem, tact*   **GREEK ROOTS** *cycl, graph*

CLUES

ACROSS

4. If one day you are famous, people might ask you for this.

5. Whole

8. You should always wear a helmet when you ride this.

9. To use things again rather than throw them away.

10. Your sense of touch

DOWN

1. Do this to learn your part in the play.

2. The lead in a pencil

3. That statue is a war _____.

6. Sports might be your favorite after-school _____.

7. A performer in a play or movie

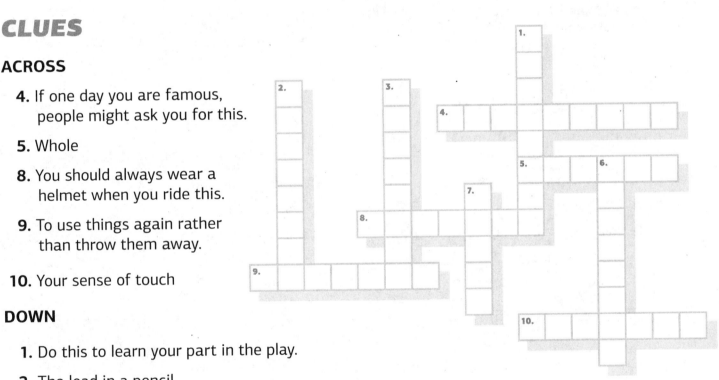

On the back of this sheet, write a sentence that includes two or more words from the puzzle.

Name _____   Date _____

Word Cards

▸ **Complete the word cards.**

▸ **Cut them out and tape or staple them to index cards.**

▸ **On the back, illustrate one word for each root.**

▸ **Add the Root Picture Card (page 58) from your teacher to the front or back of the card.**

LATIN ROOT act

Means _____

Words I know with *act:*

1. *Action* means _____

2. *Activity* means _____

3. *React* means _____

4. Other words I know with *act:*

_____

GREEK ROOT cycl

Means _____

Words I know with *cycl:*

1. *Cyclone* means _____

2. *Recycle* means _____

3. *Unicycle* means _____

4. Other words I know with *cycl:*

_____

GREEK ROOT graph

Means _____

Words I know with *graph:*

1. *Autograph* means _____

2. *Graphic* means _____

3. *Graphite* means _____

4. Other words I know with *graph:*

_____

GREEK ROOT mem

Means _____

Words I know with *mem:*

1. *Commemorate* means _____

2. *Memorial* means _____

3. *Memorize* means _____

4. Other words I know with *mem:*

_____

LATIN ROOT tact

Means _____

Words I know with *tact:*

1. *Contact* means _____

2. *Intact* means _____

3. *Tactile* means _____

4. Other words I know with *tact:*

_____

The Root of Baseball

SKILL Identify roots and cognates
NUMBER OF PLAYERS Whole class
OBJECT OF THE GAME To name a cognate for a given root and use it correctly in a sentence

MAKE THE GAME CARDS

1. Duplicate the blank game cards (page 54) on card stock and give two to each student. (You can also hand out index cards.) Have students select roots from Units 3 and 4 (pages 25 and 30). For each root, have students write the root and meaning of the root on one card and three or four cognates on the other.

2. Collect the root cards and then the cognate cards. Set the cognate cards aside. Mix up the root and definition cards and place them facedown in a pile.

PLAY THE GAME

1. The class plays as a single team, with the teacher as pitcher. Designate corners of the room as home, first, second, and third bases. The pitcher sits in the middle of the room.

2. Students line up along the side of the room by home base. The first batter steps up to the plate.

3. The pitcher turns over the first card and reads the root and its definition. The batter selects single, double, triple, or home run. For each base, the batter must name a cognate and use it correctly in a sentence—one for a single, two for a double, three for a triple, and four for a home run. If the batter is correct, he or she advances. If the batter is incorrect, the student scores an out. Players move from base to base as batters correctly name cognates and use them in sentences. Each player who returns to home plate scores a point for the class. Play until all students have had a turn at bat.

4. Record the date and number of runs and outs. Play again later in the week and compare the scores.

MORE WAYS TO PLAY

▸ Instead of reading the roots and definitions, use the cognate cards. Batters name the root and what it means.

▸ Use roots from Units 1 through 4.

Name _____ Date _____

Time Flies

Read the clues. The Latin or Greek root is hidden within the clues. Look for the word parts that are the same in the boldface words.

1. Latin root for *make*. Many things made in a **factory** are **manufactured**. An **artifact** is something made long ago that is of cultural or historical interest. A **benefactor** is someone who makes or provides something good for others.

Latin root for *make*: ____ ____ ____
                              7

2. Greek root for *star*. **Astronomy** is the study of outer space. An **astronaut** is a space traveler. An **asterisk** is this star-shaped symbol: *. An **asteroid** is a large rock in space that is smaller than a planet.

Greek root for *star*: ____ ____ ____
                         6

3. Greek root for *earth*. **Geography** is the study of the surface of Earth. **Geology** is the study of rocks, soils, minerals, and other things that make up a planet. **Geometry** is the study of points, lines, angles, curves, surfaces, and solid shapes.

Greek root for *earth*: ____ ____ ____
                         8   2

4. Latin root for *break*. As a volcano **erupts**, hot magma from the center of the Earth breaks through the surface crust. When you break into someone else's conversation you **interrupt** them. People who are **bankrupt** are unable to pay because they are "broke."

Latin root for *break*: ____ ____ ____ ____
                           5   1

5. Greek root for *shape*. A tadpole goes through **metamorphosis** to become a frog, completely changing shape and form. Something **amorphous** has no shape. When an image on the computer screen **morphs**, it changes from one thing to another.

Greek root for *shape*: ____ ____ ____ ____ ____
                         3   4

BONUS Write the numbered letters in the spaces below to spell out the Latin phrase that means *time flies*.

____ ____ ____ ____ ____ ____   ____ ____ ____ | ____
 1   2   3   4   5   6   7   5   8   1

On the back of this sheet, explain what the expression "time flies when you're having fun" means to you.

Name _____   Date _____

Cloze Call

Write the root that completes the unfinished word in each sentence.

1. Building a dam can change the _____**graphy** of an area.

2. The _____**ured** steam pipe damaged the street above it.

3. Most clothing is **manu**_____**tured** in other countries.

4. In the movie, a tiny green alien suddenly _____**ed** into a giant blue monster!

5. An _____**eroid** headed toward Earth would burn up in the atmosphere.

Use an answer from above in a sentence of your own.
Underline the word with the root in your sentence.

_____

_____

Draw a picture for your sentence to help remind you of the word's meaning.

Name _____ Date _____

Word Search: Mystery Idiom

Read the clues. Write the answers on the lines.

  1. This Latin root means *break*. ___ ___ ___ ___

  2. This Greek root means *shape*. ___ ___ ___ ___ ___

  3. This Greek root means *star*. ___ ___ ___

  4. This Latin root means *make*. ___ ___ ___

  5. This Greek root means *earth*. ___ ___ ___

Circle your answers in the puzzle. Search down, across, and on the diagonal.

F	A	C	B	R
O	N	S	A	U
F	I	D	T	P
E	G	E	O	T
M	O	R	P	H

BONUS On the lines below, write the letters you did not circle in order from left to right, top to bottom.

___ ___ ___ ___   ___ ___ ___ ___

This Latin phrase means "in good faith, genuine." When you make an effort in good faith, you try your very best. Use the Latin phrase in a sentence of your own.

_____

_____

Name _____   Date _____

Root Crossword Puzzle

Read the clues. Use the roots in the box below and what you know about them to complete the puzzle.

> **LATIN ROOTS** *fac, rupt*   **GREEK ROOTS** *ast, geo, morph*

CLUES

ACROSS

2. The science that studies outerspace

3. The name for this symbol: *

7. A scientist who studies the surface of the Earth

9. His kitten _____ from a cute ball of fluff into a snarling tiger.

10. The study of curves, angles, points, and lines

DOWN

1. In a small town, the local _____ might employ most of the people.

4. The parade had to stop because protestors _____ the marchers.

5. A piece of pottery from ancient Greece

6. A tadpole goes through this to turn into a frog.

8. You have no money. You're broke.

Unscramble the shaded letters to spell the Latin root for *star*. Find the root in *constellation*, a group of stars—for example, the Big Dipper.

Latin root for *star*: ___ ___ ___ _L_ ___ ___

Name _____   Date _____

Word Cards

▸ **Complete the word cards.**

▸ **Cut them out and tape or staple them to index cards.**

▸ **On the back, illustrate one word for each root.**

▸ **Add the Root Picture Card (page 59) from your teacher to the front or back of the card.**

GREEK ROOT ast (also astr)

Means _____

Words I know with *ast/astr*:

1. *Asterisk* means _____

2. *Astronaut* means _____

3. *Astronomy* means _____

4. Other words I know with *ast*:

_____

LATIN ROOT fac

Means _____

Words I know with *fac*:

1. *Artifact* means _____

2. *Factory* means _____

3. *Manufacture* means _____

4. Other words I know with *fac*:

_____

GREEK ROOT geo

Means _____

Words I know with *geo*:

1. *Geology* means _____

2. *Geography* means _____

3. *Geologist* means _____

4. Other words I know with *geo*:

_____

GREEK ROOT morph

Means _____

Words I know with *morph*:

1. *Amorphous* means _____

2. *Metamorphosis* means _____

3. *Morphing* means _____

4. Other words I know with *morph*:

_____

LATIN ROOT rupt

Means _____

Words I know with *rupt*:

1. *Bankrupt* means _____

2. *Erupt* means _____

3. *Interrupt* means _____

4. Other words I know with *rupt*:

_____

Name _____ Date _____

It's a Secret

Read the clues. The Latin or Greek root is hidden within the clues. Look for the word parts that are the same in the boldface words.

1. Latin root for *head*. The **captain** runs the ship. Washington, D.C., is the **capital** of the United States. The **capstone** is the stone at the top of a wall or other building. To **decapitate** is to remove the head.

   Latin root for *head*: ____ ____ ____
                           5

2. Latin root for *health*. **Sanitation** crews pick up trash to keep the streets clean and the town healthy. Mentally healthy people are **sane**. People with severe mental illness are said to be **insane**. The sneeze-guard shield at a salad bar keeps the food **sanitary**.

   Latin root for *health*: ____ ____ ____
                             1

3. Greek root for *love*. **Philanthropists** show their love for humanity by supporting charities and other good works. A **philosopher** is someone who seeks or loves wisdom. People who attend **philharmonic** performances appreciate good music.

   Greek root for *love*: ____ ____ ____ ____
                        6   7   8   9

4. Latin root for *row* or *rank*. The **order** of events take place one after another. **Ordinal** numbers show rank: first, second, third, and so on. **Ordinary** means not special, or of no special rank. Something extra-special, out of the ordinary, is **extraordinary**.

   Latin root for *row* or *rank*: ____ ____ ____
                                 4   3   10

5. Latin root for *short*. An **abbreviation** is a short form of a longer word. A **breve** is the curved symbol for a short-vowel sound. The saying "**Brevity** is the soul of wit" means that to be clever, one should use only a few well-chosen words.

   Latin root for *short*: ____ ____ ____ ____
                          2   11

BONUS Write the numbered letters in the spaces below to spell out the Latin phrase that means "secretly" or "in a private way."

____ U ____   ____ ____ ____ ____
1   2   3   4   1   5

BONUS BONUS This Pennsylvania city is known as the City of Brotherly Love.

____ ____ ____ ____ ____ ____ ____ ____ ____ ____ ____ ____
6   7   8   9   5   10   11   9   6   7   8   5

Name_____ Date _____

Cloze Call

Write the root that completes the unfinished word in each sentence.

1. The class lined up and filed out in an _____**erly** manner.

2. The **ab**_____**iated** term for President of the United States is POTUS.

3. The cleaning crew _____**itizes** the hospital every day.

4. In legends, the _____**ospher's** stone can turn lead into gold.

5. The _____**tain** said, "Full speed ahead."

Use an answer from above in a sentence of your own.
Underline the word with the root in your sentence.

_____

_____

Draw a picture for your sentence to help remind you of the word's meaning.

Name _____   Date _____

Word Search: Mystery Root

Read the clues. Write the answers on the lines.

1. This Latin root means *health.* ____ ____ ____

2. This Latin root means *rank.* ____ ____ ____

3. This Latin root means *head.* ____ ____ ____

4. This Greek root means *love.* ____ ____ ____ ____

5. This Latin root means *short.* ____ ____ ____ ____

Circle your answers in the puzzle. Search down, across, and on the diagonal.

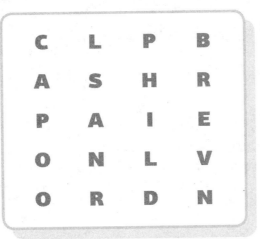

C	L	P	B
A	S	H	R
P	A	I	E
O	N	L	V
O	R	D	N

BONUS On the lines below, write the letters you did not circle in order from left to right, top to bottom.

___ ___ ___ _G_ _A_

This Latin root means the opposite of *brev*. Complete this Latin idiom with the word.

Ars ____ ____ ____ ____ ____ , *vita brevis.*

Ars means "art." *Vita* means "life." What does the idiom mean?

_____

Name _____ Date _____

Root Crossword Puzzle

Read the clues. Use the roots in the box below and what you know about them to comp
the puzzle.

> **LATIN ROOTS** *brev, cap, ord, san*   **GREEK ROOT** *phil*

CLUES

ACROSS

3. A scholar who works to understand the nature of life

4. *Mr.* is the _____ form of the word *mister.*

6. Run-of-the-mill, not special

8. The first letter of your name should be this kind of letter.

9. The symbol used to indicate a short-vowel sound

10. A number like *first, second, fifth, tenth,* and *so on.*

DOWN

1. Someone who supports charities to help others

2. The first mate and the crew salute him or her.

5. An extremely mentally ill person might be described this way.

7. We washed our hands before handling the food in order to be _____.

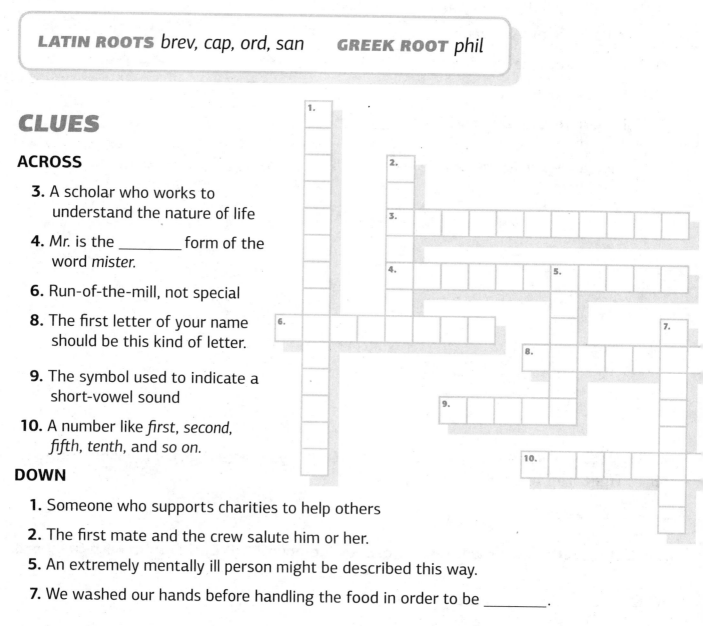

On the back of this sheet, write a sentence that includes two or more words from the puzzle.

Name _____   Date _____

Word Cards

▸ **Complete the word cards.**

▸ **Cut them out and tape or staple them to index cards.**

▸ **On the back, illustrate one word for each root.**

▸ **Add the Root Picture Card (page 60) from your teacher to the front or back of the card.**

LATIN ROOT *brev*

Means _____

Words I know with *brev*:

1. *Abbreviate* means _____

2. *Breve* means _____

3. *Brevity* means _____

4. Other words I know with *brev*:

_____

LATIN ROOT *cap*

Means _____

Words I know with *cap*:

1. *Capital* means _____

2. *Capstone* means _____

3. *Captain* means _____

4. Other words I know with *cap*:

_____

LATIN ROOT *ord*

Means _____

Words I know with *ord*:

1. *Extraordinary* means _____

2. *Ordinal* means _____

3. *Ordinary* means _____

4. Other words I know with *ord*:

_____

GREEK ROOT *phil*

Means _____

Words I know with *phil*:

1. *Philanthropist* means _____

2. *Philharmonic* means _____

3. *Philosopher* means _____

4. Other words I know with *phil*:

_____

LATIN ROOT *san*

Means _____

Words I know with *san*:

1. *Insane* means _____

2. *Sane* means _____

3. *Sanitation* means _____

4. Other words I know with *san*:

_____

Sorting Hats

SKILL Identify root of cognates
NUMBER OF PLAYERS Whole class
OBJECT OF THE GAME To sort cognates by their roots

MAKE THE GAME CARDS

1. Label four different hats or other containers with roots. Duplicate the blank game cards (page 54) and give four to each student. (You can also hand out index cards.) Have students select a cognate for each root you've chosen and write the cognates on their game cards.

2. Collect the cards, mix them up, and divide them into two or more equal piles, one for each team. To differentiate the teams' cards, use markers to color-code them—for example, red dots for one team and blue dots for another.

PLAY THE GAME

1. Place the sorting hats in different corners of the room.

2. Divide the class into two or more teams.

3. Designate a row of desks or a table as each team's home base. Select a captain for each team.

4. Give team captains a group of color-coded cards. On your signal, the captain distributes the cards and players run to sort the words by root, placing the cognate in the correct hat. When all team members have distributed their cards, they run back and sit down at their home base.

5. Teams score points for each correctly sorted cognate. The first team to return to home base first wins five bonus points (provided they have sorted their cards correctly).

MORE WAYS TO PLAY

▸ Write roots on the outsides of individual envelopes. Give envelopes and a group of cognates to pairs or small groups. Have them sort the words in the correct envelopes.

▸ Use roots and cognates from Units 1–5.

▸ Time the sorting activity. Play again later in the week, challenging students to better their scores and times.

Name _____   Date _____

Who, Me? Yes, You!

Read the clues. The Latin or Greek root is hidden within the clues. Look for the word parts that are the same in the boldface words.

1. Greek root for *word*. A **dialogue** is an exchange of words. A **monologue** is a long speech given by one actor. The **prologue** is the introduction that comes before the main story. To **apologize** is to say you are sorry.

   Greek root for *word*: ____ ____ ____

2. Latin root for *draw tight*. **Strict** rules keep everything under control. To **restrict** is to hold something within fixed limits. A boa **constrictor** is a snake that suffocates its prey by squeezing it tight.

   Latin root for *draw tight*: ____ ____ ____ ____ ____ ____
   <u> 1 </u>   <u> 3 </u> <u> 2 </u> <u> 4 </u>

3. Latin root for *greatest*. To **maximize** is to make the most of something. The **maximum** is the very most something can be. A **maxim** is a short saying that makes the most of a few words to state a proven truth or general principle.

   Latin root for *greatest*: ____ ____ ____
                <u> 8 </u>

4. Latin root for *new*. A **novel** is a new story. A **novelty** is something that is new, different, or unique. A **novice** is someone who has just started to learn or do something. A **nova** is a star that suddenly increases in brightness for a short time.

   Latin root for *new*: ____ ____ ____
          <u> 5 </u>

5. Latin root for *drive*. To **propel** is to move forward. When you feel **compelled**, you feel you must do something. To be **expelled** is to be sent or driven away. Something that **repels** you drives you away. **Propellers** drive a plane or boat forward.

   Latin root for *drive*: ____ ____ ____
        <u> 7 </u> <u> 6 </u>

BONUS Write the numbered letters in the spaces below to spell out the Latin maxim that means "know yourself."

____ ____ ____ ____ ____   ____ ____ _I_ ____ ____ _U_ ____
 1   2   3   4   5   4   6   7   1   8

This phrase is considered a maxim, an important truth. On the back of this sheet, explain why is it important to know yourself.

Name _____ Date _____

Cloze Call

Write the root that completes the unfinished word in each sentence.

1. The kids **apo**_____**ized** for hitting the ball through the window.

2. The jeweled case was a _____**elty** no one could resist.

3. They sprayed insect **re**_____**lent** before the barbecue.

4. The army **re**_____**ed** soldiers to the base.

5. The _____**imum** score you can earn is ten.

Use an answer from above in a sentence of your own.
Underline the word with the root in your sentence.

_____

_____

Draw a picture for your sentence to help remind you of the word's meaning.

Name _____   Date _____

Word Search: Mystery Root

Read the clues. Write the answers on the lines.

1. This Latin root means *drive.* ____ ____ ____

2. This Greek root means *word.* ____ ____ ____

3. This Latin root means *draw tight.* ____ ____ ____ ____ ____ ____

4. This Latin root means *new.* ____ ____ ____

5. This Greek root means *greatest.* ____ ____ ____

Circle your answers in the puzzle. Search down, across, and on the diagonal.

P	L	C	A	S
E	V	O	E	T
L	A	T	G	R
E	M	V	M	I
P	O	A	T	C
N	O	R	X	T

BONUS On the lines below, write the letters you did not circle in order from left to right, top to bottom. This Latin phrase means "Let the buyer beware."

____ ____ ____ ____ ____   ____ ____ ____ ____ ____

What does this warning mean to you?

_____

Name _____   Date _____

Root Crossword Puzzle

Read the clues. Use the roots in the box below and what you know about them to complete the puzzle.

> **LATIN ROOTS** *log, max, pel, strict*   **GREEK ROOT** *nov*

CLUES

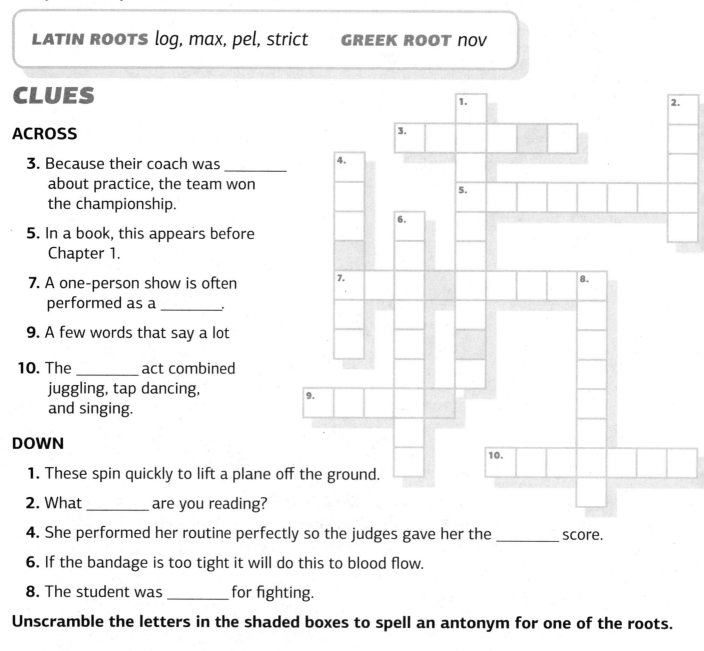

ACROSS

3. Because their coach was _____ about practice, the team won the championship.

5. In a book, this appears before Chapter 1.

7. A one-person show is often performed as a _____.

9. A few words that say a lot

10. The _____ act combined juggling, tap dancing, and singing.

DOWN

1. These spin quickly to lift a plane off the ground.

2. What _____ are you reading?

4. She performed her routine perfectly so the judges gave her the _____ score.

6. If the bandage is too tight it will do this to blood flow.

8. The student was _____ for fighting.

Unscramble the letters in the shaded boxes to spell an antonym for one of the roots.

____ ____ ____ ____ ____

The mystery root means _____

Name _____   Date _____

Word Cards

▸ **Complete the word cards.**

▸ **Cut them out and tape or staple them to index cards.**

▸ **On the back, illustrate one word for each root.**

▸ **Add the Root Picture Card (page 55) from your teacher to the front or back of the card.**

GREEK ROOT log

Means _____

Words I know with *log*:

1. *Apologize* means _____

2. *Dialogue* means _____

3. *Prologue* means _____

4. Other words I know with *log*:

_____

LATIN ROOT max

Means _____

Words I know with *max*:

1. *Maxim* means _____

2. *Maximize* means _____

3. *Maximum* means _____

4. Other words I know with *max*:

_____

LATIN ROOT nov

Means _____

Words I know with *nov*:

1. *Nova* means _____

2. *Novel* means _____

3. *Novelty* means _____

4. Other words I know with *nov*:

_____

LATIN ROOT pel

Means _____

Words I know with *pel*:

1. *Expel* means _____

2. *Propel* means _____

3. *Repel* means _____

4. Other words I know with *pel*:

_____

LATIN ROOT strict

Means _____

Words I know with *strict*:

1. *Constrict* means _____

2. *Strict* means _____

3. *Restrict* means _____

4. Other words I know with *strict*:

_____

Name _____ Date _____

Seize the Day!

Read the clues. The Latin root is hidden within the clues. Look for the word parts that are the same in the boldface words.

1. Latin root for *beginning*. The **origin** of a river might be a spring high up in the mountains. An **original** story is completely new, not copied or based on something else. The first or native people of a place are **aboriginal** tribes.

   Latin root for *beginning*: ____ ____ ____ ____
   <u>   5   </u>

2. Latin root for *no*. A **negative** answer to a question is "no." To **renege** on a promise is to go back on your word and not do what you promised to do. A **renegade** is someone who chooses not to follow the laws and customs of a group or society.

   Latin root for *no*: ____ ____ ____
         3

3. Latin root for *small* or *less*. The **minimum** is the least amount. A **minor** is a person younger than 18 and not considered an adult. **Minus** is the mathematical operation of taking away, resulting in less. To **minimize** is to reduce or make smaller.

   Latin root for *small* or *less*: ____ ____ ____
         6

4. Latin root for *order*. Soldiers follow the **commands** of their officers. To **demand** is to order someone to do something. Something that is **mandatory** is something that must be done.

   Latin root for *order*: ____ ____ ____ ____
       1   4

5. Latin root for *give*. To **contribute** is to give of your time or money to a cause or effort. To **distribute** is to give to others something they need. A **tributary** is a river that flows into or gives its water, to a larger river.

   Latin root for *give*: ____ ____ ____ ____
       2

BONUS Write the numbered letters in the spaces below to spell out the Latin maxim that means "seize the day."

<u> C </u> ____ ____ <u> P </u> ____   ____ ____ ____ ____
   1   2   3   4   5   3   6

What does this maxim mean to you?

_____

Name _____   Date _____

Cloze Call

Write the root that completes the unfinished word in each sentence.

   1. His _____***ative*** attitude made him no fun to be with.

   2. The ***ab***_____***inal*** people were forced off their lands.

   3. The President of the United State is the ***Com***_____***er*** in Chief.

   4. Each class ***con***_____***uted*** crafts they made for the fundraiser.

   5. Only a small _____***ority*** of the class didn't want to go on the trip.

Use an answer from above in a sentence of your own.
Underline the word with the root in your sentence.

_____

_____

Draw a picture for your sentence to help remind you of the word's meaning.

Name _____ Date _____

Word Search: Mystery Idiom

Read the clues. Write the answers on the lines.

1. This Latin root means *less.* ____ ____ ____

2. This Latin root means *give.* ____ ____ ____ ____

3. This Latin root means *no.* ____ ____ ____

4. This Latin root means *order.* ____ ____ ____ ____

5. This Latin root means *beginning.* ____ ____ ____ ____

Circle your answers in the puzzle. Search down, across, and on the diagonal.

M	A	N	D	N
O	U	M	E	M
T	R	I	B	I
R	O	I	U	N
N	N	E	G	O

BONUS On the lines below, write the letters you did not circle in order from left to right, top to bottom.

____ ____ ____ ____ ____ ____   ____ ____ ____

Which Latin word means *number*?

_____

Name _____   Date _____

Root Crossword Puzzle

Read the clues. Use the roots in the box below and what you know about them to complete the puzzle.

> **LATIN ROOTS** *orig, neg, min, mand, trib*

CLUES

ACROSS

2. The leader _____ your attention.

4. League before the majors

5. She _____ cards to each player.

6. Many fairy tales _____ in France.

8. The Ohio River is a _____ of the Mississippi River.

9. I have a poster, but the _____ hangs in the museum.

DOWN

1. His vote against the rule _____ her vote for it.

3. English and math are _____ courses.

4. The _____ desserts are just a single bite.

7. The opposite of positive

Unscramble the letters in the shaded boxes to spell an antonym for the root that means the opposite of beginning.

____ ____ ____ ____ **means** _____.

Write the mystery root to complete the sentence.

The *ex_____inator* sprayed for bugs.

Name _____   Date _____

Word Cards

▸ **Complete the word cards.**

▸ **Cut them out and tape or staple them to index cards.**

▸ **On the back, illustrate one word for each root.**

▸ **Add the Root Picture Card (page 62) from your teacher to the front or back of the card.**

LATIN ROOT mand

Means _____

Words I know with *mand:*

1. *Command* means _____

2. *Mandatory* means _____

3. *Demand* means _____

4. Other words I know with *mand:*

_____

LATIN ROOT min

Means _____

Words I know with *min:*

1. *Minor* means _____

2. *Minimum* means _____

3. *Minus* means _____

4. Other words I know with *min:*

_____

LATIN ROOT neg

Means _____

Words I know with *neg:*

1. *Negative* means _____

2. *Renege* means _____

3. *Renegade* means _____

4. Other words I know with *neg:*

_____

LATIN ROOT orig

Means _____

Words I know with *orig:*

1. *Aboriginal* means _____

2. *Origin* means _____

3. *Original* means _____

4. Other words I know with *orig:*

_____

LATIN ROOT trib

Means _____

Words I know with *trib:*

1. *Contribute* means _____

2. *Distribute* means _____

3. *Tributary* means _____

4. Other words I know with *trib:*

_____

Vocabulary Password

SKILL Identify roots from exemplars
NUMBER OF PLAYERS Pairs
OBJECT OF THE GAME To name the root when given a list of cognates
ADDITIONAL MATERIALS Minute timer

MAKE THE GAME CARDS

1. Duplicate the blank game cards (page 54) and give two or more to each student. (You can also hand out index cards.) Have students write a root at the top of each card and list four cognates for it below.

2. Collect the cards and mix them up. Give each player ten cards facedown in a pile.

PLAY THE GAME

1. Player 1 gives the word clues. Player 2 will guess the root.

2. Player 1 starts the timer and reads the list of cognates on the first card. Player 2 names the root and its meaning. If Player 2 is correct, he or she gets the card. If Player 2 is incorrect, Player 1 keeps the card. Player 2 can choose not to guess and say, "Pass." Player 1 then goes to the next card.

3. Play continues for one minute. At the end of one minute, players count the number of cards for which Player 2 has correctly named the root.

4. Players switch roles and use the second pile of word cards. Player 2 starts the timer and reads the list of cognates to Player 1. Players score one point for each correct word.

MORE WAYS TO PLAY

▶ Use roots and cognates from Units 1–8.

▶ To play as a whole class, have students line up. Set the timer for 3 minutes. From the first card, read the list of cognates to the first student in line. (You may also choose a student to be the reader.) The student names the root and its meaning. If correct, he or she gets the card and moves to the end of the line. If the player says, "Pass", read him or her the next set of words. When the timer goes off, tally the class score by counting the number of cards students collected. Set aside the used cards. Play again so that each student gets a turn. Challenge students to improve the class score by naming more roots in the same amount of time.

Game Cards

See directions for review games on pages 20, 31, 42, and 53.

UNIT 1 ROOT PICTURE CARDS

aqua/aqu	bio	gen	mater/matr	spec
aqua/aqu	bio	gen	mater/matr	spec
aqua/aqu	bio	gen	mater/matr	spec
aqua/aqu	bio	gen	mater/matr	spec
aqua/aqu	bio	gen	mater/matr	spec

Unit 2
cogn, loc, nat, ped, sign

UNIT 2 ROOT PICTURE CARDS

cogn

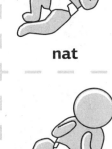

loc

nat

ped

sign

cogn

loc

nat

ped

sign

cogn

loc

nat

ped

sign

cogn

loc

nat

ped

sign

cogn

loc

nat

ped

sign

UNIT 3 ROOT PICTURE CARDS

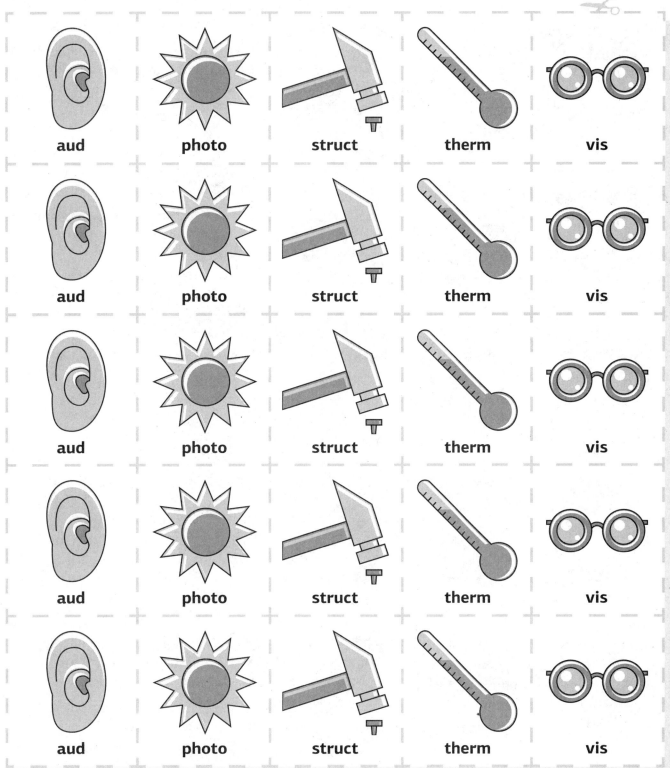

aud	photo	struct	therm	vis
aud	photo	struct	therm	vis
aud	photo	struct	therm	vis
aud	photo	struct	therm	vis
aud	photo	struct	therm	vis

Unit 4
act, cycl, graph, mem, tact

UNIT 4 ROOT PICTURE CARDS

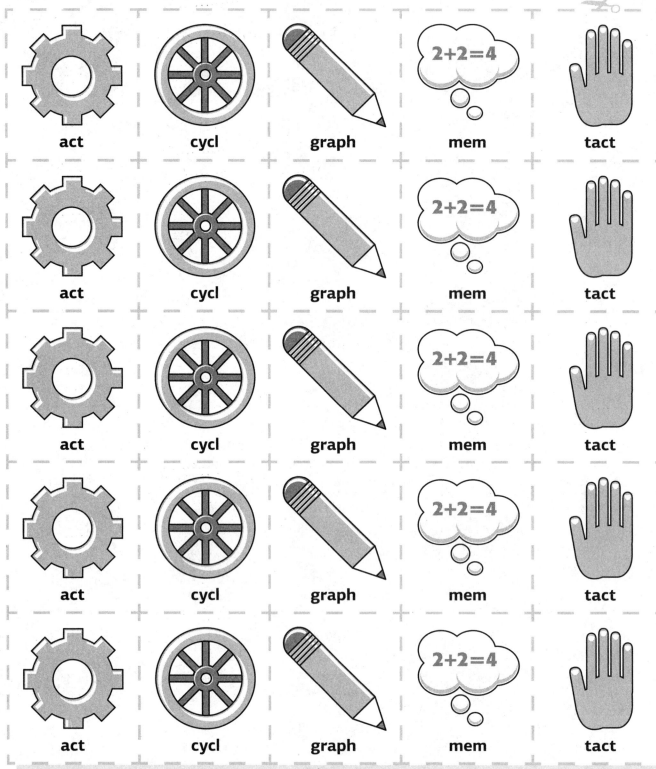

UNIT 5 ROOT PICTURE CARDS

ast/astr	fac	geo	morph	rupt
ast/astr	fac	geo	morph	rupt
ast/astr	fac	geo	morph	rupt
ast/astr	fac	geo	morph	rupt
ast/astr	fac	geo	morph	rupt

Unit 6
brev, cap, ord, phil, san

UNIT 6 ROOT PICTURE CARDS

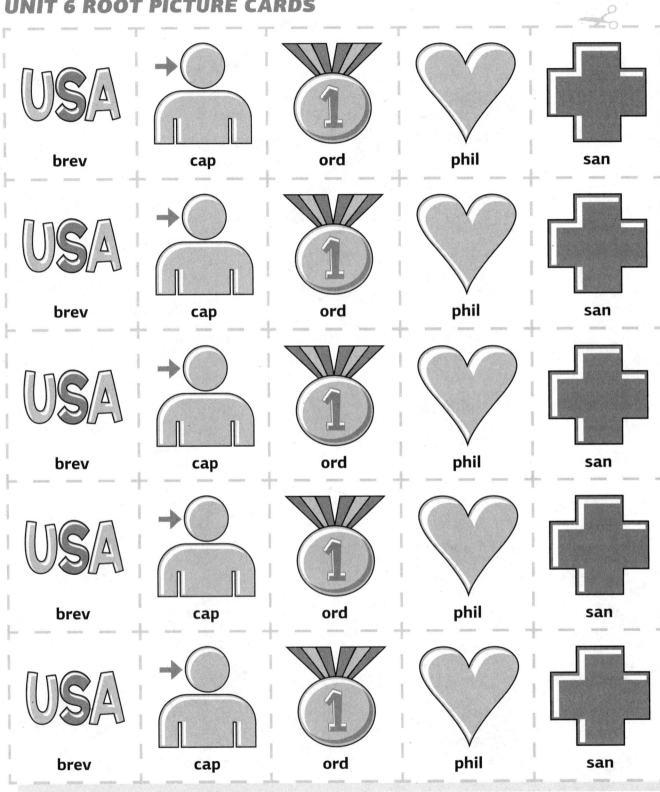

brev	cap	ord	phil	san
brev	cap	ord	phil	san
brev	cap	ord	phil	san
brev	cap	ord	phil	san
brev	cap	ord	phil	san

UNIT 7 ROOT PICTURE CARDS

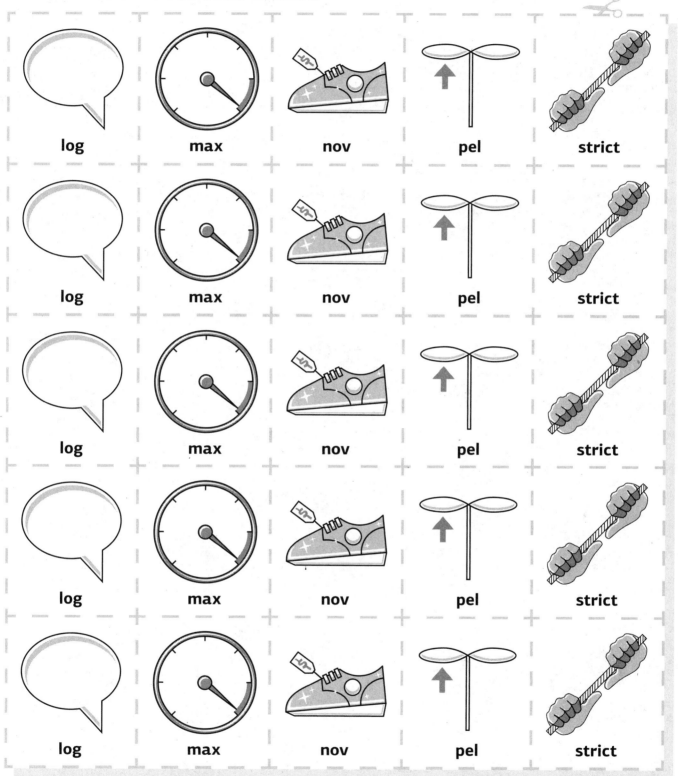

UNIT 8 ROOT PICTURE CARDS

mand

min

neg

orig

trib

mand

min

neg

orig

trib

mand

min

neg

orig

trib

mand

min

neg

orig

trib

mand

min

neg

orig

trib

Unit 1

PAGE 10
1. mater 2. aqua 3. gen 4. bio 5. spec
Bonus: E pluribus unum; plus, unit; many: pluribus; one: unum

PAGE 11
1. biology 2. maternity 3. generation
4. aqualungs 5. spectators
Sentences and pictures will vary.

PAGE 12
1. aqua 2. bio 3. mater 4. spec 5. gen
Bonus: Et cetera; etc.; Sentences will vary.

PAGE 13
Across: 1. spectacle 4. aquarium
8. generation 10. maternity
Down: 2. aqua 3. maternal
5. generate 6. biology 7. inspector
9. progeny
Sentences will vary.

Unit 2

PAGE 15
1. loc 2. sign 3. nat 4. cogn 5. ped
Bonus: Cogito ergo sum
Bonus Bonus: *bi* means *two*; biped, bicycle

PAGE 16
1. pedals 2. incognito 3. signature 4. local 5. naturally

PAGE 17
1. cogn 2. sign 3. ped 4. loc 5. nat
Bonus: Ad lib (ad libitum); Sentences will vary.

PAGE 18
Across: 4. recognize 6. nation 8. innate
9. recognizable 10. dislocated
Down: 1. biped 2. local 3. significant
5. pedestrian 7. signal
Sentences will vary.

Unit 3

PAGE 21
1. vis 2. therm 3. struct 4. aud 5. photo
Bonus: Vice versa; audiovisual.

PAGE 22
1. photogenic 2. vision 3. thermostat
4. construct 5. inaudible
Sentences and pictures will vary.

PAGE 23
1. therm 2. struct 3. photo 4. aud 5. vis
Bonus: Ad nauseam; Sentences will vary.

PAGE 24
Across: 1. photography 3. vision 4. thermos
5. invisible 8. structure 10. construction
Down: 2. auditorium 6. photocopy
7. thermometer 9. audio
Sentences will vary.

Unit 4

PAGE 26
1. cycl 2. act 3. mem 4. tact 5. graph.
Bonus: Mea culpa
Bonus Bonus: biography; "life written down"

PAGE 27
1. contact 2. recycling 3. commemorates 4. actors 5. graphologist
Sentences and pictures will vary.

PAGE 28
1. act 2. graph 3. cycl 4. mem 5. tact
Bonus: Per diem; Possible answers: substitute teaching, acting, singing, construction work; Sentences will vary.

PAGE 29
Across: 4. autograph 5. intact 8. bicycle
9. recycle 10. tactile
Down: 1. memorize 2. graphite
3. memorial 6. activity 7. actor
Sentences will vary.

Answer Key

Unit 5

PAGE 32
1. fac 2. ast 3. geo 4. rupt 5. morph
Bonus: Tempus fugit; Answers will vary.

PAGE 33
1. geography 2. ruptured 3. manufactured 4. morphed 5. asteroid
Sentences and pictures will vary.

PAGE 34
1. rupt 2. morph 3. ast 4. fac 5. geo
Bonus: Bona fide; Sentences will vary.

PAGE 35
Across: 2. astronomy 3. asterisk
7. geologist 9. morphed 10. geometry
Down: 1. factory 4. interrupted 5. artifact 6. metamorphosis 8. bankrupt
Bonus: Stella

Unit 6

PAGE 37
1. cap 2. san 3. phil 4. ord 5. brev
Bonus: Sub rosa; Philadelphia

PAGE 38
1. orderly 2. abbreviated 3. sanitizes
4. philosopher's 5. captain
Sentences and pictures will vary.

PAGE 39
1. san 2. ord 3. cap 4. phil 5. brev
Bonus: Longa; Great art outlives the artist (literally: art is long, life is short).

PAGE 40
Across: 3. philosopher 4. abbreviated
6. ordinary 8. capital 9. breve 10. ordinal
Down: 1. philanthropist 2. captain
5. insane 7. sanitary
Sentences will vary.

Unit 7

PAGE 43
1. log 2. strict 3. max 4. nov 5. pel
Bonus: Scito te ipsum; Answers will vary.

PAGE 44
1. apologized 2. novelty 3. repellent
4. restricted 5. maximum
Sentences and pictures will vary.

PAGE 45
1. pel 2. log 3. strict 4. nov 5. max
Bonus: Caveat emptor; Answers will vary.

PAGE 46
Across: 3. strict 5. prologue 7. monologue
9. maxim 10. novelty
Down: 1. propellers 2. novel 4. maximum
6. constrict 8. expelled
Bonus: Micro; tiny, smallest

Unit 8

PAGE 48
1. orig 2. neg 3. min 4. mand 5. trib
Bonus: Carpe diem; Answers will vary.

PAGE 49
1. negative 2. aboriginal 3. Commander
4. contributed 5. minority
Sentences and pictures will vary.

PAGE 50
1. min 2. trib 3. neg 4. mand 5. orig
Bonus: Numero uno; numero

PAGE 51
Across: 2. commands 4. minor
5. distributed 6. originate
8. tributary 9. original
Down: 1. negated 3. mandatory
4. mini 7. negative
Bonus: *Term* means end; exterminator